Liber IV

LIBER IV
A NOMAD'S GRIMOIRE

by

Paul Waggener

OPWW005

CONTENTS

Author's Note   7

Prologue: Pilgrimage   11

July 2nd, 2017. Day 1.   30

July 3rd, 2017. Day 2.   39

July 4th, 2017. Day 3.   47

July 5th, 2017. Day 4.   55

July 6th 2017. Day 5.   61

July 7-8, 2017. Days 6 and 7.   71

July 9 2017. Day 8.   109

July 10, 2017. Day 9.   112

July 11th and 12th, Days 10-11.   116

July 13, 2017. Day 12.   121

July 14 And 15, 2017. Days 13 and 14.   123

July 16th, 2017 Day 15.   125

July 17, 2017. Day 16.   129

July 18, 2017. Day 17.   133

July 19, 2017. Day 18.   139

July 20, 2017. Day 19   143

July 21, 2017 Day 20   147

July 22, 2017 Day 21.   149

July 23, 2017 Day 22.   151

July 24, 2017. Day 23   153

July 25, 2017. Day 24.   159

July 26, 2017, Day 25.   161

July 27, 2017. Day 26.   163

Epilogue: An Exhortation To Adventure   171

AUTHOR'S NOTE

The book in your hands can be read and implemented in more than one way. The first is as a narrative of a month long motorcycle trip from the east coast of America, to the west, and all the way back again, and the sights, insights and thoughts that came from that experience.

The second is the book that exists within it and alongside it—a nomad's grimoire created along the highway piece by piece—integrating a system of sigils with a practice that is laid out for the discerning eye within the flow of the greater work.

Absorbed in a form of exosmosis from somewhere beyond the borders, the visions from along the way seemed to seep from a place where the sun met the highway, behind the moon, between the stars. Psilocybin and silence, miles and miles and midnight meditations on the void itself.

The prose, that is, the events and experiences that make up the bulk of the text exist in the same fashion as clothing on a beautiful woman—to accentuate and stimulate the imagination, to enhance the form that lies beneath it. But just as the garments are not the woman, and a glove is not the hand, the narrative and experience is a covering over the hidden hand that moves it.

This work could not have been written without the aid of

and

and it is to those harmful and helping spirits this work is dedicated.

Marijuana
POWERFUL LADY -
THE BREATH OF SHIVA -
THE OUTLAWS PRAYER -

GREEN TEMPLE-
ASTRAL YGGDRASIL-
: PRAY:

WE RESTORE THE TEMPLE
TO ITS GLORY

Psilocybe
:ING: ◇ RESIDES IN THE
HEART OF THE STUDENT/SEEKER. THE HARVEST
OF WISDOM WITHIN PROVIDED BY THE TEACHER —
:HOLY HOLY HOLY: FRIEND OF THE WITCH, FLESH
OF THE GODS —

PROLOGUE: PILGRIMAGE

"Once, Samanas had travelled through Siddhartha's town, ascetics on a pilgrimage, three skinny, withered men, neither old nor young, with dusty and bloody shoulders, almost naked, scorched by the sun, surrounded by loneliness, strangers and enemies to the world, strangers and lank jackals in the realm of humans. Behind them blew a hot scent of quiet passion, of destructive service, of merciless self-denial."

Hermann Hesse, *Siddhartha*

IT BEGAN AS AN IDEA between myself and a long-time friend, a flicker of a concept, mentioned in passing, that became an obsession: cross the United States from one salt water to the other, and back again. For some involved in the discussion, it would be a grand adventure, a conquest for glory and a way to reconnect and recharge.

For me, it was a pilgrimage. A ritualized mission of endurance and drawn out meditation through the discomfort, using the motorcycle as a spiritual vessel of austerity and ascesis. A way to travel physically as an external focus point for the traveling occurring within, mapping out the unknown regions and exploring some of the more lonesome frontiers of the inner wilderness.

The planning of the trip became secondary to the idea of simply going—being on the move with little to nothing in the way of personal possessions, and only a vague idea of "West" as a certain direction. This has always been the way I've done things—I have trusted in the process itself, and let things proceed and unfold in the way they will, while exerting pressure or influence in the areas I can or decide to. Both ritual and life itself proceed this way for me, and my burning faith in the righteousness of the entire process is only shaken in the blackest of moments.

Those times of great darkness are a crucial part of it all, the twin pillars of Trial and Ordeal reducing one either to dust and ashes and rust, or burning away the dross of comfort and weakness. Like the redwood forest I have always longed to see, the fires can act as a purifying agent if our intention, awareness and will remain true.

Maps were drawn up and discarded, lines criss-crossing one another in twisting sigils of eternal motion, serpents of potential and the unknown embracing one another and doubling back on themselves, Ouroboros. It was decided that we would simply choose our route and destinations the day of each ride, and by that general consensus make our eventual way from one end of this American Empire to the other and back in a long, lazy loop that would describe its way through lowland and high prairie, southern woodland to burning desert.

At the start, it was just my brother Sam and I, planning our way through another adventure like we always had since we were kids. I've known Sam Carnes since I was 8 or 9 years old, when we met outside a church our parents were attending. We decided from the get-go that we didn't like each other, and words turned into punches as they do sometimes, and that was our first encounter. He won, and I remember the stung pride from the beating I took.

Somewhere after that, we were at a church potluck, and a forced conversation ensued. We realized we shared a surly streak, and that our dislike for those around us was a sort of bonding agent between us. An uneasy alliance grew into a friendship that has lasted my whole life since.

In the years following, Sam and his brother Nathan became my lifelong friends and constant inspiration for a life of experience and adventures.

Sam is what people mean when they say "tough as nails," both in mind, body and demeanor.

Stubborn as a mule and sharp as a knife, Sam will growl about how stupid you are while helping you out of yet another jam—the most loyal guy I've ever met, and easily the most capable.

This is one fella who won't go out with his boots off—he's kayaked the southern rivers to the ocean, fought a convict in the streets with a machete, lost a leg from a gunshot, traveled from one end of the country to the other several times, rolled the dice and stayed in the game.

When Sam came into this world, they broke the mold. There won't be another like him.

Slowly the traveling party began to emerge, with some falling off during the early stages of the idea, and others making dedicated plans to join either from the beginning or at some later date, meeting up with the riders out west of the Appalachian forest from which we would begin our journey.

At the last minute, my brother Matthias decided to join the crew, fresh out of a shit marriage, with no plans and nowhere really to go. I talked him into buying a bike (it didn't take much), and he threw in his lot with Sam and I, much like he'd been doing his whole life.

More on Matthias later, but suffice it to say, I couldn't have been happier to have him along, and looking back, I'm glad he was.

From its inception, there was a certain heaviness on the ride itself. All knew that it would test the resolve and reliability of both of man and machine—breakdowns and exhaustion would play a real role in the making or breaking of everyone involved. The spiritual nature of the journey was expressed and shared by most, looking for some greater truth from the doing of the thing.

The night before the convoy rolled out, a ritual was performed at my tribe's sacred land, which we in the Wolves call "Ulfheim," or "Wolf-home," invoking the name and protection of the Unknown Rider who sits astride his own spiritual vessel, that of the cosmos itself:

> "*Oh Hooded One, who sits astride the cosmos—*
> *Performing the holy rituals of eternal movement,*
> *At war with the forces of entropy, stagnation and cold.*
> *Furious one, whose kingdom is the burial mound—*
> *Give strength, speed and freedom to us*
> *The ghosts and devils of your wild funeral procession.*
> *From our first ragged breath to our dying day,*
> *Throw wide the gates, and make straight the way.*"

On the way down the hill toward the ritual, that sabbath of wolves, I sang the word "home" over and over in an older tongue of my people, in repetition so that I could be heard by the spirits of that place, that they might work their strange and invisible will to bring me back to these woods, intact, or in death.

Not one given to great superstition, I have used plants and meditation to see these spirits directly out there—pale women sitting up in the crotches and boughs of poplar and beech, just there at the edge of the eye and the mind, calmly nodding their assent at your passing.

There's a feeling of belonging and welcome there that I know all my brothers and sisters in my tribe feel, and many of have made deals and compacts with the genius loci of our spiritual home. It's something not easily explained to outsiders, but I know that when I go down for the last time, and there's no picking myself back up—whatever remains of me will walk at the edge of the firelight when my brothers sing songs of power and tell the stories of our friendship together.

Two individuals unexpectedly decided to join us for the first day's ride, one of my best friends Devin, and his old lady, and so our number as we pulled out of the gravel drive was 6—correlating to the :K: rune of the Elder Futhark, a fitting one after the prior evening ritual's closing statement "in a world of ashes, let us be the flame." Gasoline mixed with the rider's blood was thrown into the fire as a blessing for our way.

During maintenance of the motorcycle before leaving, I mixed my blood into the oil that was the lifeblood of the horse I would ride, and pondered the mysteries of the :EHWAZ: rune, that of the horse and rider, and the symbiotic relationship they shared. The motorcycle is the horse of our day—the idea that somehow the mechanical is less sacred or "natural" than any other thing that is manifested on the planet is a small way of thinking. Man has created complex satellite systems out of materials pulled from the earth and the tree, dirt and swamp.

He pulls black liquid death up from the unseen depths of the world and refines it into a fuel source that is used to power machines of speed and murder, attack jets and tanks, the motorcycle and the spacecraft.

The mechanical can be seen as one way in which the universe can be understood, just as one may meditate on the tree in order to grasp the ideas of cosmos. Each small piece moving in a dance of complementary functions to drive the entire—accelerator pump, piston, and the power of lightning running through the cordages. The cylinder is inseminated with this anti-seed, ejaculated into that womb from the carburetor or fuel injector, and then quickened as the piston drives through the cylinder, and spark creates that explosion from whence movement comes. The process of intercourse and impregnation played out by pieces of metal forged by the hand of man in a beautiful and roaring display.

Concrete and steel, wood and water, barbed wire, graveyard or rocket fuel—all exist here and so all are part of this sacred whole. None is more holy than the other, none more "natural" or unnatural.

On this journey, an extremely light load out was desirous. What does one need for a month on the road? How little can you get away with in this life? The philosophy of minimalism has been one that is very close to my heart, and following the concept has led me to practice a lifestyle of what some might consider extreme simplicity, especially when it comes to the amount of physical possessions I choose to (not) own.

I live, at the time of this writing, in a small home in the woods, a repurposed construction site office trailer that I tore the guts out of and finished with pine, wired up to a small generator and placed out on a few acres I was able to purchase due to this simplicity of lifestyle. My wife and I live there in the peace and quiet that only comes from rural living, and the headspace one can achieve while away from the filth and

noise distractions of city life has been excellent. There are, of course, certain challenges that can arise from an "off-grid" situation, but we welcome these as part of the experience and deal with them as they come along.

Due to the consistent paring down of material objects, a gear load-out that was small enough to fit into two tiny saddlebags and one dry bag was not difficult. For a one month excursion, the following is what I saw as "necessary," including some aspects of excess that would allow me to do so in relative comfort:

- Blanket/bedroll, attached to the front forks.

- Protein bars/dried meat to cut down on costs.

- 2 pairs of jeans (the seat and "crotch" section of these saw rapid wear and tear and facilitated some repairs along the way)

- Two shirts, one short sleeve, one long sleeve, and a hooded sweatshirt for chilly nights and mornings (even in the summer time, a few areas of high desert made me pleased I had brought this along)

- Extra socks (crucial for avoiding "boot rot," although even with these, wearing my boots sometimes for days at a time without removal still did a number on my hooves)

- Phone, charger (used external battery supply purchased for 50 bucks on Amazon that I charged occasionally at longer stops

- Chromebook for writing, cost about 130 dollars and holds an excellent charge for writing in the woods as I am doing at this moment

- Tool roll (took sockets and ratchet plus wrenches for all the different size bolts and nuts on the 1998 Harley Sportster I'm

on, plus zip ties, electrical tape, adjustable wrench and a few other odds and ends and extra fasteners)

- Tent (small motorcycle tent that sets up either off a tree or directly off your motorcycle. Small and compact)

- Self-inflating air mat (I have found this to be instrumental in getting any kind of decent sleep on less than optimal ground. Sleep is a major part of putting solid miles in during the day with relative safely)

- Contact lenses, toothbrush, deodorant and normal "overnight" stuff.

That was it. After packing everything up, I found that I hadn't even filled the allotted space, and couldn't think of anything else I really needed. After two weeks on the road, I decided that I'd done a pretty good job, and wanted for nothing on the road, and that I might have even been solid with less.

The final days leading up to getting long gone seemed to take an eternity. Last minute checks of bike and gear, sorting out cash allocation and all the rest built up into a kind of anxious pull, like a dog choking itself on its own leash. I relaxed and let go, knowing that this one life is all we get—dashing always forward into some imagined future leaves us with no head for the present, and the marrow of the present is often ignored for the empty promise of something greater on a non-existent horizon.

The eastern philosophies talk about sorrow and grief stemming mainly from an over-attachment to the results of our actions, rather than performing the action for its own sake, and this has resonated with me more and more strongly the older I get.

The future is not real, it only exists as potential and expectation, often misplaced, or clung to so hard that we are never happy with the actual outcomes. If we perform our actions out of the sheer lust for life, and the satisfaction that can come while watching our dog play in the woods,

or a leaf on the winds in fall, we have accomplished something that most never realize—and a deep feeling of contentment can come from this.

On the other hand, greatness is not often achieved through zero forethought or without an understanding of cause and effect. Will is brought to bear on past, present and future, through seeing the whole concept of time as a fabric, a weave which we can view from above.

This kind of knowledge can be developed by an attention to our actions on a deeper level, seeing how the moving parts of this world interact with one another, and applying the knowledge gained to each new experience—allowing us to live in the present with a thorough understanding of how the future is likely to play out based on our movements and choices and the psychology and modes of the other humans we come into contact with. This is a lifelong endeavor of bringing ourselves always into the current moment and acting deliberately and thoughtfully, with intention and insight, each new situation teaching us an applicable lesson.

This has been my experience with motorcycles as well. At first, a huge unknown conglomeration of parts and mysterious sequences, slowly understood more and more through time spent on and with one, through breakdown and repair, riding and resurrecting. Gradually, the system is worked out and known, not hypothetically but by direct experience, hands-on praxis with the occult secrets of the machine. The whole world, the whole cosmos, must work this way as well, because what is above is like that which is below—this is one of the poetic laws of the universe that I have always found to be astoundingly true, and have applied over and over again with clear success.

Tomorrow, we can deal with tomorrow. Today, this hour, this minute, this moment—we will exist here, and breathlessly walk our path with courage and pure intention.

: CROSSROADS :

:THE MASTER: WAITS AT THE
CROSSROADS - A PHYSICAL,
AND SPIRITUAL DEAL AND
EXCHANGE - BOLD OF HEART AND BRIGHT
OF MIND WILL NOT GET CHEATED IN THIS
DEALERS GAME - THE ETERNAL COVEN-
THE PROMISE OF THE SERPENT.

JULY 2ND, 2017. DAY 1.

ON THE FIRST DAY of the journey, I found myself passing through places that brought me back to different locations in the timeline of my life, specifically some of those spots that I had test ridden and purchased old motorcycles, mounts of the past, now long gone, sold, traded, or ridden into the ground like warhorses whose hearts failed after glorious times together.

I got into motorcycles later in life than a lot of my friends, and didn't own or ride my first one until my early twenties. An early 90's model Kawasaki Ninja 250 with a beat up body and unreliable carburetor that would only seem to run for a few rides at a time before requiring another tear down. I knew nothing about mechanical work at the time, and wouldn't for a good while after, but my older brother told me if I could get the bike working again, it was mine. I remember those first few rides like they were yesterday.

The thrill of going what felt like a million miles an hour in the wind, and the exhilaration of how much it felt like flying. I learned how to shift and clutch on some old back roads near our house and a few hair-raising heart pounding cruises up through the twists and turns of the Blue Ridge Mountains near my town, and eventually got my license endorsement.

I rode the hell out of that first bike, pushing it to its limits and taking it for a few long rides down the east coast, until Bike Week in Myrtle Beach finally killed it for the last time I was willing to work on it, and I abandoned it disgustedly in a roadside parking lot and made it back home in the chase vehicle. Back then I didn't have any technical knowledge, but what I lacked even more was patience. Riding bikes, especially older ones, is tough on folks with no patience, and no ability to control their temper, and that was certainly me at the time.

I still struggle with my temper and patience, but in a decade or so, I have calmed down a bit, and realized that a broken down bike isn't a dead bike. You've got to put in the time on the wrench to earn your righteous rides, and the gods of the machine don't love a quitter.

My second ride was an old Kawasaki KZ 305, a little cruiser with some more mechanical gremlins that I could never get running great, but that bike got me around all over the place, and was the first one I had that really felt like "me." Olive drab rattle can paint job, metal seat pan with no upholstery, and a goat skull tie wired onto the triple tree to set off the wasteland look.

Eventually bills and poverty got in the way of my relationship with that one, and I sold it for a ridiculously low amount to pay my rent. I remember, even after only having it for a year, how incomplete I felt without a bike, and I vowed to never go without one again. This bike taught me about making the vehicle an extension of yourself—that what we create with our hands and raw materials is a high act of the magical will, making our environment a product of our own vision.

If a man can only be known by his body of work, it follows that we should treat everything within our sphere as an opportunity to hone our crafts, beautify and make monstrous, constructing legendary songs, items, pieces of sigilized material given a life and doom by our hand and heart. A bike is no different, and certainly no less than any other thing, and a conveyance can certainly be a satisfying work to undertake.

I have had a lot of bikes, but I still remember the feeling of inquiring after an ad I saw right after it was run, advertising a Harley Davidson at a price I thought couldn't be real. In this case, too good to be true wasn't, and by the next morning I was throttling down the highway on my first Harley. There's definitely something about them, mainly due to the importance placed on them by the American biker culture that has spread all over the world since the early days of

riding, racing, and club life—as a kid watching one percenters fly down the road on those roaring machines, it was never a Honda I aspired to own.

I've had great experiences on those bikes from the far east, but as soon as I rode an HD, I knew I'd be on them for life. That first one was just an old 883, well maintained by a friendly old guy who had plenty of money and other vehicles to justify letting this one go for next to nothing. I took it on a five day trip with some friends down the east coast, and sold it once I got home. I immediately put the cash straight across for a beat up 1200 Sportster a friend owned and had let go to rust and ruin.

There's something of an alchemical process for me in the buying, fixing, trading or selling process that is one of the things I really enjoy about bikes. A distillation process of moving further and further toward some golden ideal of the "perfect bike." I'm not there yet, but every year I get a little closer. Just like the personal transformation process, it's a constant movement in the direction that is correct for you, realized a little bit more every day that you remain consistent with your goals, consonant with your aims and methods and modes of being. There is a mysterious and profound truth in everything that exists if we allow ourselves the space and time to see it and explore it. This ongoing work of attempting to achieve the impossible, that being perfection, is the praxis of attaining the Great Work. But before we can do this—we must know where we are going.

This journey, in so many ways, reflected that concept for me—one cannot simply wander off in any random direction each day and arrive at his goal. There has to be a greater framework being built—both a goal, and a process with which that can be realized.

That first day we made salt water in a small North Carolina town, and after immersing our bodies in the Atlantic, we placed our rear tires in the water, a symbolic and ritualized beginning to our great undertaking. A look was shared amongst those assembled, which was heavy with purpose, eagerness and a lust for life and motion that felt like it was being fed straight from the motor that powers the cosmos itself. We ripped the throttle and roared into destiny, "like a band of gypsies, we go down the highway—insisting that the world keep turning our way."

The salt water dried on our skin in the hot wind, and as the sun set it was huge, coming up over a big bridge, spilling its blood all over the highway like a benediction for our little band of wayfarers.

JULY 3ʳᴰ, 2017. DAY 2.

LIT OUT FROM GARNER, N.C. with the sun still coming up after a night of great company with a true brother Anthony (it's his hand behind some of the sigils you'll see through this book), good smoke and better music. The day was a blur of sun on Highway 40, until massive black clouds began to form and the rain kicked in somewhere up in the Smokies and became a blinding monsoon, driving cars, trucks, and us off the road.

I got separated from the rest in the downpour and took refuge under a hotel awning to pour buckets of rain water out of my boots for what wouldn't be the last time on this first leg. While I sat there waiting for the rest of the guys, I started to think about other times on the road, other crews I'd run around with, both road tripping across the country and playing music out on the road with friends long gone. I thought about the last long drive I'd made out west, knocking down shows with a long-time brother who I'd known since he was 15, lost two years back to the needle and the spoon.

In the song I wrote to memorialize this last trip I had made with him, and the conversations we'd had along the way about bad choices, the women we had loved and had to let go, our wars with the black dog of depression, and a thousand other things, I had written:

> *"This old prairie is like an ocean—you stop moving, and you'll drown son*
> *And beneath those crushing waves, the endless weight of memory, you'll go down.*
> *These old highways will leave you empty, and so will I if you just let me*
> *And at the vast, wide end of it all, we just go staggering out of life*
> *And sing, Oh, Death—come claim me."*

That friendship, and the loss of it, taught me a lot, and it was a lesson I wish I'd never had to learn. I miss him just about every single day, and have often woke up from dreams where I'd made different decisions and avoided the way things went down in the end. Maybe somewhere, from those dreams, those universes exist in which I made the right choices and the guilt and sorrow are gone, but I have to live in this one with the reality of it.

I miss you, Njal, and I hope somewhere out there you've found that peace that passes out of understanding. I'll see you on down the road, far from silver and sunshine.

In the years following his death, I have tried to honor that friendship by righting wrongs in other areas and paying closer attention to the time I invest in my relationships with other people, the responsibility one has to those he has chosen to bind himself together with. Friendship must be approached with a sincerity and purpose, like anything else, and one of those aspects is that we must look out for them. Being out on the road with these guys, even in the first two days, seeing a brother lay his bike down, semis change lanes without seeing them, cycles sliding across flooded highway—you've got to look out for each other in this world, because it will swallow up even the strong.

There is an old saying from the Viking age, "a man's back is bare without his brother," and I take this to heart. At our strongest, alone, we are still alone. We may think of ourselves as "a rock, an island," but in truth, humans can be fragile creatures, there and then gone in the blink of an eye. What we can accomplish through tying our fates to other strong and vital humans is staggering, and these times of tribal bonding through adversity and risk drive the point home. The feeling one has when knowing that these other powerful people are watching over you and pushing for the best outcome is one that humbles and creates a strong feeling of gratitude and honor, strangers in a strange land, back to back against the entire world outside of that holy circle.

Even with road dogs, the long journey and those nights out in unknown towns, abandoned fields, and silent woods still produces a feeling of high lonesome—an ache right in the center of everything that you can never fix or remove. As a younger man, I first came to understand this feeling. I had brothers growing up, and when I moved away from them all for the first time, there was a hollowness that I felt like a hammer to the stomach. My mid-teens were spent in almost complete isolation, living out days at a time in my room in the grips of a powerful depression that I could never seem to separate myself from. I would wake up feeling like a boulder was on top of me, and a grey and very bleak horizon loomed behind every word and action.

I did what I could to combat it, reading, listening to music, writing endlessly, angsty stuff on an old manual typewriter, lifting weights in the garage being one of the only times I'd leave my room other than to stalk the neighborhood at night like a hungry ghost. Like many other youths before me, I discovered a lot of writers that became a big influence on me, even if I don't read some of them anymore. Henry Rollins, Nietzsche, Bukowski, Bret Easton Ellis, Kerouac, Hunter S. Thompson.

Under my dad's insistence, I read my way through the "Great Books of the Western World" series and did what I could to absorb everything from Kant to Socrates, Dante, Machiavelli, Shakespeare, Melville, Herodotus— turning in reports each week on what I had retained. I was always a reader, from a very young age, and had a pretty decent grasp on grammar. I remember winning a spelling bee when I was in kindergarten against a team of 5th graders, even though I bombed in the real event from a bad case of stage nerves.

Those teenage years were a really dark and lonesome time for me, and in a lot of ways, set the stage for my later years. I never have gotten over this feeling of "being alone in a crowded room," and I'm sure a lot of people can relate. Depression has remained a life-long foe, that I have made war against through weights, martial arts, hallucinogens and an obsessive process of self-evaluation and adjustment, and I have won a lot of those battles—but that deep, crazy, awful lonesome feeling is one I have had to make peace with, and in some ways, maybe even tentative friends.

Turning your devils into your friends can be a difficult but powerful endeavor. I don't really believe in weak points, just opportunities to do the Work—a character flaw can become a strength if one can explore it enough to find its use, or to turn it on itself through rigorous exercise. I was a very shy kid, and in a lot of ways I still am, and so I have compensated for that by challenging myself to work outside of my comfort zone nearly all the time. When we are comfortable, there is no risk, and as they say, without risk, no reward. One of the biggest challenges in life is never becoming so comfortable that we stop playing the game, stop rolling the dice and jumping into the fray. Once we have stopped doing that, forward progress has ceased, and we are effectively no longer living, just existing.

Spent the rest of the night in the hotel, getting dry, and hanging out with some acquaintances who had come down from Indiana and Tennessee to meet up in person. Some Jack Daniels was passed around and some laughs were had, and we were on our way.

JULY 4TH, 2017. DAY 3.

GOT A LATE START in the morning, with the rain a relentless force that had zero interest in our travel plans. Decided there was nothing to it but to do it, and headed out on the road, bedraggled and a bit miserable, but determined to make forward progress.

Somewhere toward evening the rain finally cleared up for a while and we cruised through small town Kentucky as the Independence Day celebrations kicked off in earnest, and the fireworks displays lit the night sky up as we'd breeze into one town like they were celebrating our arrival, and continued as we rolled on through and gone, as though they were overjoyed to see us leave.

People still trip out a bit on dirty, tattooed madmen ripping motorcycles out across the country, and there is an easy to spot difference between someone who likes bikes out for a cruise, and a group of road beaten dogs, tall bags strapped down to sissy bars, out of state plates from a long haul away, eyes on fire and tired at the same time. There's a certain anxiety I see it produce in small towns amongst the locals, as if at any time you will drag their women away by the hair to a cave outside of town, or start a dispute at a gas pump and burn the whole town. And to be honest, there is that impulse lurking in there somewhere, that smoldering coal of the truly barbaric, that one feels when out on the road far from home.

In a way, it is similar to the feeling of the lucid dream, when one becomes aware that he is dreaming while still dreaming. I have often thought how strange it is that in those dreams, I have often turned immediately to an unchecked viciousness, a heady blend of rapine and murder, exhilarating in its utterly savage freedom. I think this is perhaps true for most, or certainly most men in the same situation. Our spirits remain brutal, though the mind may be civilized.

Like Wolf Larsen from Jack London's amazing "Sea Wolf," I have often thought in moments (or years) of pessimism that the human being has little purpose beyond the strong eating the weak to simply survive, and that the lust for domination and violence is inseparable from the human experience, because it forms the bedrock of what it means to be an animal.

Finding some meaningful way to navigate this concept and utilize it when called for is crucial to being able to operate freely in this world, in this time. Men who cannot control it wind up in prison or the early grave, and men who cannot call upon it become victims or forever subservient to those who have it. Law and government has ensured that these types of men are kept in check, and that the weak are protected from the strong through a complex and infinitely litigious system of rule and legal repercussion for the smallest offence, the shallowest dip into the river of bloody action.

Author and creator of Conan, Robert Howard believed that beneath the civilized exterior of every man was "the ape, roaring and red-handed," and I don't disagree, but I believe it has been buried much more deeply in some than in others.

For every local who eyes you with distrust and fear, though, there is the other kind. Those that shake their head in admiration when you tell them where you're from and where you're going. Old timers checking out the bikes and getting a far-off look with a "man, I wish I was going with y'all." These are our kind of people, and we always share a few words with them and take away a little piece of their story with us. Adventurers, men who have done enough to have stories layered through their years worth the telling.

There are also those who will only ever "wish they were going." These types will go down into the darkness of unwritten histories, forgotten names that the centuries will wash over as though they had never been—the Stygian shores of time unmarked by their timid footstep. This is the most meaningless life of all, and a shameful waste of the mathematical improbability of existence. That we are even here is nearly impossible—that we should waste seconds, hours, days and years in a state of steady discontent and repetition is, to me, a blasphemy against life. Make legends. Be a legend. Let the myth of your life overflow with story and song, and leave something behind that others feel quickening their pulse and driving them to hot, righteous action—all else is dust.

The rain kicks up again on and off in western Kentucky and we hit the end of our patience at Land Between the Lakes and make camp and a fire.

: TENT/TEMPLE :

: ꞇɛnꞇ/ꞇɛmplɛ :

FOR THE ROAD WEARY, THE TENT AND
TEMPLE ARE ONE. SOLITUDE. REFLECTION
SHELTER - ':SOL: ENERGY DRAWING IN
AND OUT WITH THE RISE AND FALL
OF YOUR SLUMBERING MIND. · ᚴ · ᚷ · ᛉ ·
MANI CHASES SOL - WE RISE AND GIVE THANKS —

My tent is my temple. Within it, I am initiated into the mysteries of the roadside prophet, and the wandering mystic. In this Temple of Change, I exist in a liminal space between worlds, and as I write, or draw, or read, I am transformed, re-emerging into the world a new creature. As a nighttime refuge, it is feminine, welcoming, and above it, the moon hangs steady in its course, 13 cycles of waning and waxing throughout the lunar year. The number is that of the :Eihwaz: rune, one of heightened consciousness, initiation, the number following after the willing sacrifice of the hanged man, and the balance between life and death, sleeping and waking, light and darkness. In this occult lodge, I travel the worlds in my mind and in my dreaming state, projecting myself through all times and places, my fetch flying hard on the wings of will. I awaken strong, electric—my internal drive fueled up and ready to hammer away, pistons striking smooth and steady.

It exists also as a break from sensory perception. Riding a motorcycle can produce a near-paranoia state of hyper awareness that becomes exhausting to the mind. Stimuli at every corner of the vision: truck creeping out from a crossing, gravel in the turn, driver changing lanes without signaling, strange rattle from the motor, missed my exit, stay awake, sun in my eyes, roll on the throttle to pass a swerving semi-truck, don't hit the rider in front of you as he brakes hard to avoid a potential crash. The brain stays awash in these things and it wears you down—this is where the bad shit happens. You get tired, over-stimulated, careless, and the bloody gods of highway and black oil open you up on their altar. There is a certain zen that occurs out there, but it comes along with a sharpened alertness—the zen happens when the alertness is there with this perfect calm when you know everything is operating smoothly. That is a rare and wonderful feeling that is often gone as soon as it envelops you, and the quiet dark within the confines of the tent are a welcome respite from that chaos. Sleep, and silence.

JULY 5TH. 2017. DAY 4.

WAKE UP SOAKED through still at 5am and hit the road before the sun rises. Within 5 minutes, my gas tank has sprung a leak and is throwing a fine fan of gasoline on my left leg, and we pull off into some tiny town whose name I can't remember for breakfast and a plan. JB Weld wins the day, and we patch the tank under the shelter of a hardware store awning. I foolishly believe this will be the end of it, and we cruise into more rain, crossing the Mississippi and Missouri, taking in the bleak ruins of Cairo, IL along the way.

Troy, MO holds a significance for us, as we are meeting another rider there, who will link up and head to saltwater with us. We link up with Cody, the as yet unsung pride of Muncie, Indiana, at his sister's house, and take a brief break before an oncoming thunderstorm prompts us to try to get out there and beat it. We don't, and as the rain starts to lash down again, my tank opens up for real, and I'm getting drenched with gas on my leg and shirt, and the wind is blowing it straight through the mouth vent of my helmet. At an underpass some 50 miles from Columbus, MO, we pass the time waiting for a tow truck, and finally drop off the bike at a Harley dealership and head to a cheap motel to wait out the night.

One of Odin's own prototypes, Cody is a wanderer, a brawler, and a magician. Gigantic red-headed Suebian juggernaut with an infectious laugh and tattooed face.

I've watched him wrestle in the woods like a berserker, and laugh just at the great big joy of being alive while floating on his back down the Snake River. He's at home with priests and whores, drunks and philosophers.

Cody is the sort of person that makes friends everywhere he goes, because he gives people something when they interact with him. He makes them feel like they're alive, and that there's all this possibility out there in the world, you've just gotta go have an adventure and find it.

He reminds people that there are still legends in this world, and that they are hanging out with one.

His whole attitude toward the civilized world is summed up in one of the things I heard him say at a big roaring fire early on in our time knowing each other:

> "Fuck a couch, and fuck a T.V. I don't need that shit."

The motel is the usual hellhole. Bullet proof glass over the teller window, hookers smoking meth outside our window, looking possessed by the devil himself. Bathtub looked like a body had decomposed in it a few weeks before, and maybe it had. Laid back, one or two beers, and done.

That road was rough and cold all day, easily the hardest miles of the trip so far, each one feeling like it lasted a year, while at the same time feeling like "the Jonah" of the expedition, the bad luck one with all the problems, making everyone wait and jamming up the schedule.

The sound of the motor and wind seem to drive out most of the thoughts that come to me while I ride, for better or worse—it is indiscriminate, blasting away recollection, regret, enlightenment, and ideas in a roar of exhaust, there and then gone as everything is shattered to pieces and falls together again. That's okay, too, this cessation of too much thinking. In Norse mythology, when the wisest individual, Kvasir, is murdered by dwarves, they claim that he "suffocated on too much knowledge." You see this all the time in the modern world, this overabundance of information leading to a paralysis of action—smartphones linked up to satellites that beam in every piece of knowledge one could ever hope for, but is generally used for hook-ups, social media and porno.

All this information putrefies into nothing more than distraction, and the synaptic highways are traffic jammed with ads, messages, bright lights, bullshit.

I don't want to be anywhere else but here. Not thinking of home or the next stop, on this pilgrimage to every nowhere I find myself. Just chasing the void and closing it all out, letting the wind howl like Rudra before the dawn of consciousness, turning everything into castles of sand that erode and blow away in the next gust. I don't care that I'm broke down, except that I want to keep moving, never stop, even if it is in a circle— that's cool; so is the universe, and the planets don't seem to mind as they do their thing.

A lot of guys want to chase pussy, or some other big empty idea that doesn't even match up to any kind of reality. I just want to chase my own tail and bite it, Ouroboros, finally figure out where I start and end, what's the measure of it all, who am I these days when it matters, where's all this deep rotting fear and loathing come from and where does it belong?

All the might and madness I've never processed, never slowed down to think about, rising up to the surface like Leviathan. It all needs sifting, filtering, burning in the furnace. I'd like to figure some things out—I'd say hope, but that's in short supply for me these days. I know the way things go, and the internal universe is a mapless country where we wander and wonder at its ever-changing vastness.

JULY 6TH 2017. DAY 5.

FIRST THING IN THE MORNING I'm down at the Harley dealership trying to figure out something for my leaking tank. We discover the leak isn't at the seam, so welding is pretty much out of the question, and searches of the usual spots are turning up absolutely nothing on Sportster tanks for sale.

The other guys join me after an hour or two, and an old guy takes notice of us messing around with the bike in the parking lot. He's a cool old-timer, and can't believe noone has helped us out yet—he blazes off somewhere muttering about friends with names like "Snotface," "Cookie," or "Sleazebag," and promises that they can help us out.

Another hour waiting around, and he returns empty handed—apparently even local legends like these are of no use today. The guys skateboard in the parking lot, drink a beer, talk to girlfriends on the phone, while I try to chase down some dubious leads on some other hometown chopper heroes who might be able to

help out. A brief diversion for a Road Challenge (Cody has a whole list of things ranging from the minorly dumb to the incredibly foolhardy each worth a certain amount of points one can rack up. Example: pay for gas inside wearing only motorcycle boots, helmet and skivvies—50 points. Slam a large sized milkshake in under 5 miles at highway speed—20 points. "Surf" your motorcycle down a busy boulevard—200 points) has me attempting to eat my height in beef jerky in one 5 minute sitting. I fail, and the nausea and stomach weirdness does nothing to alleviate the bad vibes of the current predicament.

After a few hours like this, I pull the tank, sand and spackle the entire underside with the gnarliest marine grade fuel tank epoxy I can find, guaranteed to set underwater and hold the Hoover Dam together. It dries and we rock out of the parking lot ready to leave Columbia behind us. Before we even get to the truck stop at the edge of town, both sides of my gas tank are

spitting gas freely through the epoxy. It's the first time on the trip I lose my temper, and I skid through the gravel on the road side, rip the fucker off and spike it into the bushes, swearing and seeing red.

This attitude is all wrong for a number of reasons that are obvious when you're not feeling it. The anger clouds the mind all up, turns you hypersensitive to any small annoyance, sets you up for more. I've had a bad temper my whole life, and have spent a lot of my late twenties and early thirties trying to really get a handle on it. My brother Matthias and my dad are the same, both controlling it to various degrees of success and failure. It's one of the things that I truly dislike about myself, because a bad temper has no real redeeming qualities as a weak point—the only strength that can be found from it is in the challenge of keeping it bridled, which is what I try to do.

Mechanical failures on the road will test that temper like nothing else, but what you gotta keep in mind is this: the anger doesn't live outside you, to be placed in there by a situation or another person. It's within, a smoldering mound of coals, that external stimulus can use against you, by throwing fuel on those coals, and creating a flare up that then completely masters you until the flame subsides or you can partially extinguish it. What a weakness for us to say, "He/She/It *made* me angry." Nothing made you angry—you were already angry. The external simply *found* that anger, and you were utterly controlled by it.

That flickering flame has been a constant for me my entire life, that white hot anger that possesses me like a devil and speaks with my mouth, acts with my limbs. It is not a source of pride, but of shame. There is a line in David Fincher's film "Seven," in which the two detectives are arguing. Somerset, in his cool, calm voice, says "We have to divorce ourselves from emotion here. No matter how hard it is, we have to focus on the details, okay?"

Mills responds, impatiently—"Man, I feed off my emotions, how's that?"

Later, after totally losing his cool and attacking a reporter, he looks over to Somerset who is quietly looking at him with disapproval. "It's *impressive* to see a man feeding off his emotions," he says, the sarcasm and disappointment dripping from his words.

The scene always stuck with me, thinking about how ridiculous it looks to see someone divorced from their reason and "feeding off their emotions." Applying these harsh criticisms on ourselves is always hard, but worthwhile—many times, what we hate in other people is a simple mirror to what we loathe about ourselves. This is not always the case, but it merits a long look.

My brother Matt walks over to where I am standing, crazed with anger at an inanimate object. He knows me well enough to not say anything, and just calmly hands me a bottle of water. Some of the other guys start working out, and as I breathe the fire out slowly through my nose, I calm. We exercise together, some good natured shit-talk ensues, and a few minutes later, a young kid from the Harley shop has a friend come through on a phone call who not only has what we need, but is willing to give it to us for free. The crew rolls over there, gets the tank, some other spare parts, and hides a 100 dollar bill from me in the kid's gas cap.

After returning to the crippled bike, we do some roadside fabrication with a mini hacksaw, some pliers, and a few pieces of bar stock, coupled with bolts pulled from a firework store display sign to make some quick and easy mounts that will work with the tank. Some extra vacuum line cut off one of the other bikes is added in, with a makeshift splitter from a pen cap in order to get the newer tank's vacuum petcock to function with the Super E carburetor. I turn the key and flick the switch and she roars to life, shiny new non-leaky gas tank mounted proudly up high on the backbone of the horse. High fives.

Speed lust kicks in, and we tear down the miles, sunset red as Judas, fades into the warm, wet blackness of mother night. We keep on riding. And riding. And riding. I start to get tired at around 1 or 2 am, shadows on the edge of the vision field, my world liquid light and white lines, pick up a gas pump at one truck stop, hang it up at another.

Pound a coffee and the caffeine sharpens you up a few minutes and bleeds into a tired anxiety, the need to keep on going and never stop. Industrial giants loom out off the sides of the highway, lit up like titanic archangels of steel and fire.

I start to feel a sense of vastness of the journey in front of us, the whole thing too big to grasp at once, too long and too heavy to see as a single entity—it'll make you start to question the whole thing, doubt yourself, feel the tug to just turn around and cash it in. I'm reminded in my sleep deprived state of the runes, or the trumps of the tarot deck.

Pieces of the big truth, all broken down into crystallized fragments, each one holding a lifetime's worth of information and illumination, bits small enough to hold in your hand or head, but as you look at them they expand and deepen into fathomless, bottomless oceans of timeless concept, written as large as your brain can hold.

They grow with you, as your experience builds, as you change and evolve as a person—you can see other angles of them that were obscured before due to your position and thought process. Ways to utilize them become clearer, and they develop a personality of their own, like trusted advisors, secondary, and tertiary brains that inform your actions and reason.

The hermit stands on the cliff, the light in his lantern beckoning the intrepid away from the city sprawled in the valley below, out into the endless night, into the wild, the frontiers of exploration and challenge. The magus must answer that call and walk away from the comfort of home, and set out on his journey, fate unrealized until he sees himself as the fool, and can laugh at the absurdity of it all layered in with the importance of doing the journey for it's own sake.

Sometime around 4 am, we crash hard at a roadside park for two hours, just taking enough time to throw sleeping bags and the ground and share a sip of whiskey before sleep takes us. Two hours later, my brother wakes us with his ever repeated mantra of: "Pow-Pow! Next one boys. The next one." He is on fire to move, to be gone, to reach a destination and be gone again. Everyone can feel that his jonesing for speed is keeping him just barely ahead of the ghosts of the past we all know he's dealing with at the time, and we try to honor that.

We get up stiff and tired, and fire up the machines again, and thrash like demons into the plains of Wyoming, finishing off the ride of 800 miles into my hometown of Cheyenne.

JULY 7–8, 2017. DAYS 6 AND 7.

THE ENDURANCE CHALLENGE is ongoing. After getting separated for a time on the highway, we meet up at the Green Door, our home away from home in Wyoming—a tiny, sleazy go-go joint that is home to some of the strangest characters (and strippers) in the west. Cold beer hasn't tasted so good in a long time, and with the knowledge we are here for a few days, we kick into excess. Messages are flown out to friends and brothers, and a crew starts to assemble of various outlaws, dirtbags, miscreants and gentleman thugs. No sleep, beer on tap, whiskey shots and good smoke turn the day and night into a blur of tits and ass and laughs. Some of the guys drop acid, and the night cranks up the dial to "motherfucker."

Jim Morrison once said "I believe in a long, prolonged derangement of the senses in order to obtain the unknown." I've never made any secret of the techniques I have used to attempt this same idea—I think that intoxicants, hallucinogens and deliriants have their place in the toolbox, and am reminded of a conversation had with a friend, a high level Jiu Jitsu practitioner and coach, who said something to the effect of, "we have to earn our ecstasies and excesses with hard work and dedication. If we engage in intoxication as a compulsive behavior, we are not 'using it,' it is using us, and will ultimately use us up."

As a younger guy, I took excesses to an extreme, and drank heavily, used drugs, especially hallucinogens and opiates, and stayed in the shadowy realms of constant, exhausting self-abuse through chemicals. I won't say there were no positive experiences, because a lot of what I went through shaped my life in ways that are inseparable from my current state, but I was an addict in every sense of the word. I never met a woman, had a mystical experience, used any drug, or felt anything that could match what alcohol produced in me. I wrote drunk, performed music drunk, worked drunk often.

There were some periods of relative sobriety that acted as ellipses between long months of total Dionysian indulgence. My ability to endure these binges became a source of pride for me—the willingness and drive to go harder, longer than anyone else I knew on a path of total death lust. Brawling, womanizing, hustling, hangover, repeat, for years.

Over time, this culminated into a thing that began to consume me, my time, my inspiration, my fire. After a divorce that ended a ten year relationship, I turned up the throttle, and turned up the bottle harder than ever. It came out of the longest time of "clean living" I had ever achieved as an adult, and the build up of anger, sorrow and despair exploded into a reckless thirst for self-destruction. I was a walking piece of human wreckage. I worked as a bouncer, a bartender sometimes, and made most of my money from playing country music, something I excelled at doing under the influence, and actually relied on. I've written very few songs in "happy" times, but whole albums in one night under Saturn's shadow and in the arms of the demon rum.

I fell back into every old, bad habit I'd ever engaged in for a calendar year. I shared my misery and broken heart aggressively on those around me, and derailed lives, broke other hearts, and let my own just keep bleeding as I poured whiskey into wounds that time never healed. Sometime in the later portion of the year, I woke up and determined to go cold turkey and get back on the path. The next day, I had the shakes so bad I couldn't hold a pen, couldn't sleep, waves of heat washing over me. I decided to go for a ride on my motorcycle, a loaner from a friend. A few miles in, I felt something like the heavy hand of doom reach into my chest. It was a feeling like no other, as if I had just gotten news that everyone I knew had died, or I'd just been convicted of murder. The pain was like every vein in my heart being ripped apart. I made it to my mom's house and threw up, blacked out, and wound up in the ER, where they told me I had suffered a heart attack from "poly-substance withdrawal."

I lay around at my apartment for a whole day after, feeling beaten and broken down, eating the little white pills they gave me, a Lorazepam prescription to "take the edge off." My mom came over and cried, and I sat there feeling like an alien, totally removed from the situation. At that point, I resolved to keep on going until the inevitable happened. As soon as she left, I walked down to the bar and took a bottle of Jim Beam, bought a pack of smokes, went back home and drank the whole thing while playing guitar.

A few friends and I had decided to take a small tour on the road, playing music out through Wyoming. We drank whiskey the whole way there, ate some speed, and knocked down three or four back to back shows in Cheyenne. By the third night, two of us were so wrecked we couldn't keep down the pre-show drinks to get rid of the shakes. We had to line up shots and beers in the bathroom, me and my pal Coyote, drink, vomit, drink, vomit, repeat, until we could hold one down and sip a beer till the buzz hit and we were high on it enough to throw down the gig.

In order to master the excess, we have to be like the blue throated Shiva, drinking the poison of the serpent and being able to transmute the toxin into something meaningful. This cannot be done through compulsive use of chemical, and cannot be seen through the haze of addiction. The self-deception that comes through addiction is a thing that blinds, shackles, and ultimately, destroys.

If one can master it, and engage in excess ritually, holding it for times when it becomes a holy expression of ecstasy, intoxication can be a tool—but only then.

Back to Cheyenne, a girl I used to know gave us the keys to her spare house and the crew stayed there while I spent some time with my wife who was visiting her mom in town.

The next day, I rode my bike out alone to a forest ritual with my brothers there in the western state, those wind-born Wolves, and watched torches flame in the night sky, strong words spoken to invoke the inspiration, powerful fungal spirits consumed from a wooden bowl mixed with sweet mead, and the moon rose full over the skeletal pines. Gifts were exchanged and reconnections made as the drink snaked its way through our veins, through our hearts, into our brains. These sacred experiences out on the edge of the world defy being placed into the confines of language.

The mushrooms did their work. The sky transformed into a slowly rotating grid of symbols and alien architecture, geometric patterns the size of the milky way slowly spiraling out there in the great nothing. The voices of my brothers combining together like serpents entwining, and the vibrations working their way out into the universe, swallowing the world and changing it.

Red bands of runes and sigils, a thousand layers deep, all moving in their own direction, their own pattern and motion, wheels within wheels, and a sound like the rushing of a great wind. Everything spiraling into the center. At the center of the galaxy, and at the center of myself, a supermassive black hole, eating everything that comes into contact with its event horizon. My brain went through it, stayed on the other side, where I gambled against space and time—how long could I remain in that massive nothingness, feel the whispers of the void, and come back intact?

A feeling when the eyes are closed like falling from a great height, it goes on and on and on and on and on and on...

1. The home we will return to. Ulfheim, Appalachia.

2. The beginning—baptism in the Atlantic.

3. The start of the trouble. Pouring rain and gasoline.

4. Midnight tow in Missouri.

5. New tank for the bike, and an offering to the highway gods.

6. Nebraska.

7. Cody.

8. Songs of loss and heartache in Cheyenne, Wyoming.

9. Now here is nowhere.

10. Down with the Union. Outside Laramie, WY.

11. Road Crew. From L.: Sam, Cody, Danny, Matthias, Me, Karl, Pest, Joe.

12. Psilocybin and silence. Wolves Ritual, Windborn country.

13. Packing up after sleeping in a graveyard in Soda Springs, ID.

14. Snakes of Christ—Snake River, Oregon/Idaho border.

15. Blood in the oil of the holy machine.

16. Giving face tattoos at Waldgang.

17. Getting my own ink from my brother Jack.

18. Shade-tree mechanics. Pest and Cody.

19. My ride for 8000+ miles. I miss this bike.

20. "Where now is the horse and his rider...?"

21. Bastard saint of the road. Thanks, Eric.

22. Stuck in the sand at the Pacific. All the way there-now back again.

23. So long to Cody. From L.: Sam, Matthias, Me, Pest, Cody.

24. Abandoned indian reservation, somewhere in the desert of
Arizona.

25. Explore Everything.

26. "Whatever you wanna call it, it's still music to me. It's there. It's the will of life."

27. "What did you go out into the wilderness to behold?
A reed shaken by the wind?
Why then did you go out? To see a man clothed in soft raiment?
Behold, those who wear soft raiment are in kings' houses.
Why then did you go out? To see a prophet?
Yes, I tell you, and more than a prophet."

28. The Highway is an endless :ISA: rune.

29. Truck stop sigils.

30. Texas is the reason.

31. The riddle of steel.
Evening with Terry Shanks.

32. Jammed up by the largest gang in the United States, Tennessee border.

33. "The Blue Ridge Mountains is where I call my home, and its among them rocks that I will lay my bones..."

JULY 9 2017. DAY 8.

A QUIET DAY after the madness of the ones prior, spent in calm and reflection.

The first true "rest day" since the trip began, and a much needed one. Thoughts of family and home, time spent with my wife and her kids, doing "domestic" things and considering their place in my life alongside all the action and struggle, challenge and ordeal.

These down-times are a strange contradiction for me, and can quickly become seen in moments of less than clear thinking as a resented prison—I shake the bars and want freedom, open road, experience. Once deep in the stretches of a personal feat, I then find myself craving the calm and silence. Life happens in these cycles, and between them is that *vesica piscis* of perfection that lasts for what seems like the blink of an eye. I am a people person crossed with a misanthrope, an idealist shot through with pessimism and a cynical worldview on humanity in general. This back and forth produces conflict and the struggle to find some kind of peace is ongoing.

Stayed in at night, writing and reading, a gift received Saturday night, a copy of "The Sea Wolf" by Jack London. As the friend stated in the inscription, I find much of myself written down in the main antagonist of the story. A mixture of the lust for life and enjoyment of adventure hexed with a deep dissatisfaction and dark worldview that is often at the surface—combatting it with a self-created "reason to live," in order to pull some meaning from this existence, even if only of my own making.

Being in my hometown is always a strange and bittersweet experience. I nicknamed it "Failure Country," on a record I wrote years ago, and it represents a lot of bad times and worse decisions. On the other hand, I grew up here, and as a kid, running the chalk bluffs around Crow Creek, looking for arrowheads and pretending to be wild Indians was high adventure of the same kind I am still chasing.

I met friends there that are still with me, my brother by choice, Sam, my best friend and longest one, who I'm riding right behind and to the left of this whole time. The best things often come from the worst, and there's no neat separation like we are always hoping for between them. Life, and the places we gauge the passing time by come to represent landmarks, monoliths of experiences that all slam together but unpack when we come through them again.

Wyoming is always big and heavy, and layered with a lot of joy and sorrow. The great plains are swept by wind, and thunderheads roll through on a scale that is well beyond gigantic, reflecting in my eyes and in my heart.

JULY 10, 2017. DAY 9.

TATTOO APPOINTMENT with a local acquaintance and member of the most notorious motorcycle club in the US—paid for a few of the lads to get one as well, a big western "T" with a crown of 5 rays above it, the Transcontinental—5 rays, 5 riders, 5 rituals. A death's head on my throat to be mindful of too much speech. "I have often regretted words I have spoken, but never regretted keeping silence."

Made a trip to a hardware store following some good conversation and painful tattooing, picking up parts and stock needed to re-do the jury rigged gas tank mounts, a headlight mount that the weld had broken off of, and some other minor fabrication. Met up with everyone at my wife's mother's house, and turned the old horse barn into our headquarters, everyone performing various work on their machines and Cody and I handing a guitar back and forth, sharing songs we'd written or learned, while my old lady grilled us up some food.

Days like these are perfection—sheltered against a big sky thunderstorm with people I genuinely care about, singing old songs, a few beers, going to sleep with my woman in my arms. These brief moments of real satisfaction are the gold that keeps life worth living, and I am overcome by a slow, steady feeling of gratefulness and calm.

I knew I had to say goodbye to my wife for the second time the following morning, and wouldn't see her for the better part of a month. Being away from her has been tough over the last three years—she's like the sister I never had, the lover I've never known, the woman I have always looked for. Time spent away from her deepens the appreciation I feel for what we have, and my love for her is intense in a way that can sometimes be agonizing.

My dad always says that love is not an emotion, but an act of the will—a feeling is fleeting, but will is a choice. I agree with him, but I am also a believer in the strange tides of fate. I have known the echoes of lives once lived, and seen in the faces of friends and loved ones the flickerings of some other time, some other place, in which I knew them and we were together, perhaps not as we are now, but the memory is real. Like walking into a place you've never been before and knowing for a certainty that you've dreamed about it or been here before in some distant reality.

In finding her, I feel as though I've only found her again, and am making up for lost time.

JULY 11TH AND 12TH, DAYS 10–11.

STARTED THE MORNING with eight riders, a few friends and associates from the area that decided to come out and do a day with us. Rode Western Wyoming and into Idaho, very rugged, harshly beautiful, Louis L'Amour country. Idaho is majestic—green, colossal spreads of emerald from mesa to mesa, shadows of the clouds spread across verdant fields. Made our way to Soda Springs, watched the geyser go off, and headed into a little juke joint where a couple locals bought us drinks and then left us to the bar. Just the crew of us in there, spending dollars on old country and Motörhead on the jukebox. Sang along and drank beer and Beam, as usual, till the cows came home.

Found refuge in a quiet graveyard, next to a tombstone that read, "A Friend To All." We felt welcomed by it, and crashed hard. Graveyards in every town are an often overlooked place of quiet reflection, a meditation on the baroque truth of "Memento Mori." Fitting for the wayward soul out on the road.

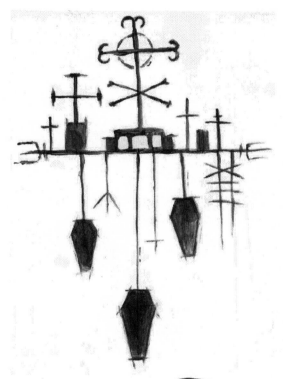

:Graveyard:

MR GRAVEYARD IS WHERE WE
ALL END UP · MEN · WOMEN ·
CHILDREN · 3 COFFINS/3 FATES
THE DEAD FEED THE EARTH ·

SOLITUDE
REFLECTION   XIII FOR THE
HOLY SILENCE   KING

***

The day began cool, and I was awakened at sunrise by the whispers of my companions telling me the local police were poking around, and we needed to get out of there. Bedrolls were hastily stowed, gear thrown together, and strapped back to motorcycles. With no other words between us, engines came to life and carried us away from another small town and out toward the horizon.

Turns out, three or four hours of sleep on the cemetery ground isn't what you'd call "optimal" for a long day's ride, and I was fighting the nods by the heat of noon. Everything starts to smear together like pastels and lose its third dimension. You sing or shout to yourself inside your helmet, until your voice sounds strange and alien, like its coming across a long distance, flat and far off.

In this tired, half awake awareness, I turned Idaho into a dreamscape as I rode, exploring areas of the subconscious while the sun beat down and melted everything into one, a weird mental state of exhaustion and calm I started calling "the sunconscious." The endless roar of engine and wind becomes a single note that drives everything else out of your mind, and you reach a place approaching true zen.

You worship god in that silence. The idle chatter at truck stop and rest area is blown away in the hard wind, the events of the night before already fading in the solar light. We live out here, endlessly. The riding becomes what you do. The times in between stand out in contrast until they are turned into some kind of sepia by the miles, and you can't remember where one day ended and another began.

Campsite at the end of the day in Baker City, OR. 3400 miles behind us, and nearly at the "halfway point" of the ride. Waiting to put our front tires in the Pacific, and then just saying "fuck it," and turning around.

We aren't out here to do anything other than make stories, to create myths before we are old men, but that future is unclear on this night. Thinking about the last time I saw my wife and being unable to shake the feeling that it was the last time I'll ever see her in this lifetime. Dwelling on death around every corner, seeing it shine in the eyes of deer on the midnight roadside, the headlights of big rigs with tired drivers barreling down at you, slipping over the double yellow.

If I die out here, I know that I lived electric, charged up and full of hell, and that I loved like no other man has ever loved a woman, fought like a rabid dog for what I held true. I could lay on the blacktop and slowly let the life bleed out and think to myself, "it was so, so good."

JULY 13, 2017. DAY 12.

GOT SOME KIND of real sleep in the blessed tent of repose and ripped the throttle, flying through Oregon—staggering views of the Columbia River as we descended from the mountains, Mt. Hood looming majestic before us, imposing, cold, grand.

Took a break somewhere and swam in the Snake River, benediction of cold water and the feeling of weightlessness after so much heaviness. These are the times that things are just exactly how they should be. Dust washes off, and so does the strain. Laughs come easy and you feel like you've got nothing on the mind or weighing on the heart.

Back on bikes in a little while and slow cruising a few dirt roads, drying off in the warm sun and wind, just feeling our motorcycles beneath us, carrying us everywhere we wanna go.

Just kept on digging that feeling and killing the miles until reaching our brother Jack's land, where a bunkhouse waited these weary travelers.

JULY 14 AND 15, 2017.
DAYS 13 AND 14.

UP IN THE MORNING for prayers to a god our ancestors called Thor out in the woods of Waldgang, weightlifting and stones hoisted up as we challenged each other to feats of strength—an old cult of strongmen, giving homage to the red god in the way he was most accustomed to in days long gone by.

These two days ran together in a blur of creek swimming, catching crawdads, invading bars and gas stations like a modern day recreation of Brando's "The Wild One." Dirty, dusty, covered in grease and oil that at this point feels like a permanent part of my skin.

The guys thrashed their Dynas on the dirt trails, racing each other in tight circles until they went down in a huge wave of dust and laughter. Cold beers and hot sun.

By this time, the drive chain on my Harley had become an unavoidable and serious issue, as the sprocket had gotten warped and the chain kept getting more and more slack, no matter how it was tightened, threatening to jump off its track and cause any kind of havoc during the ride.

A few phone calls later and a guy named Eric got in touch, saying he had the parts we needed and a shop they could be installed in Portland. We had intended to avoid the big cities for the most part, but at this point, we needed the fix, and had to do whatever the situation called for.

Fell out early on Saturday night to the sound of coyotes, those night time wanderers of the in-between, tricksters and song-dogs. I am reminded of dear friends back home, and feel lucky to be out here in the middle of a "grand adventure."

JULY 16TH, 2017 DAY 15.

WOKE UP EARLY for coffee and some last laughs with the Cascadian Wolves crew, ready for the road but reluctant to leave good friends behind.

It's an easy cruise to Portland from our friend's property in Eastern Oregon, and we pull our bikes into Eric's garage, cluttered with dirtbikes and old Harleys, including his flat black Shovelhead, easily the coolest bike seen all trip.

Eric is a true saint of the road. He has the parts I need to convert back to a belt drive. He has good conversation and an easygoing demeanor as we put the bike on his lift and start pulling it apart. His laugh is genuine and often, and I immediately like him (and not just because he is saving my ass out here!), and wish we had more time to spend in his company.

The Harley is fixed, solid, and howls back to its purpose—we fly across town to drop in at Rose City Strip, Portland's most notorious strip club, owned by our pal Mason, and a definite oasis in the hipster wasteland of Portland, Oregon.

We swap stories with our friend while naked women writhe to death metal, Snaggletooth spreading across one wall and infamous photos of some of black metal's original outlaws adorn the others. Salt water is calling, however, and this close to our purpose, we are all restless and raring to make it to Lincoln City, the next stop on this hell-ride, and the one that marks a successful run from one salt to the other.

Everyone in that club seemed to want to drop what they were doing and roll outta that dark club with us, and who could blame 'em? The day in, day out gets to be a grind that few souls were meant to endure. As Townes said, "It'll crush you down—down into nothin'."

I don't know what I'd do with myself if there wasn't always the option to roll, to ramble, to throw the dice on the uncertain game and take the risk. Up the ante. Push it to the next level. Home is for recovering, for training the mind and body, to prepare for the next great step out into the unknown—it's not a place I want to simply exist in from now until death, a constant repeating of day after day. At the thought of that, the bullet is already in the gun for me. An overdose of the mundane, needle straight to the vein. Can't do it.

They stay. We ride on. It's our road, and not theirs. Our story to tell, in which they can have as much space as their part deserves.

Night comes down cold as hell, the ocean wind kicking up and chilling us all to the bone, to our great surprise in the middle of summer. We dressed for where we were, not where we were going, but it doesn't even matter. We crank those throttles with numb hands and swear awful curses at the wind and chill at the top of our lungs to forget the sting of it.

Lincoln City at last. I honor our achievement with a nice room, view of the ocean under the dark sky, big, vast, lonesome, and sad.

The ocean always makes me feel an immense sorrow, a complete aloneness that is hard to put into words. I walk down there, and spend some time in contemplation and quiet melancholy, midnight comes and goes, and it's time to celebrate at a casino bar, where we toss back some whiskey and talk about plans for the future and what the next big adventure will be, while my brother chats up some girls who are in town for the night.

It feels good to have made it this far, but the knowledge is shot through with the realization that although we have made it across the continent, we still have thousands of miles to go, and some of the most inhospitable landscape in North America to cross before we will see home again.

JULY 17, 2017. DAY 16.

THE MORNING DAWNS chill and windy, and I head down to the beach to make a mad dash into the freezing waters of the Pacific. The cold takes my breath away, hard surf fighting against me—the shock of it wakes me all the way up, all the way alive, air, trees, water, animals—the gulls calling and wheeling overhead, the salt spray on the breeze, the driftwood on the beach. Smell, taste, see, feel, experience. Those little moments come like a thunderbolt into the conscious mind.

The crew decides we need to ride the bikes all the way down the sand to the water itself and baptize the tires in the ocean, so we do, getting a few bikes stuck in the deep wet sand in the process and shredding one drive belt to pieces for the sake of "completion." There's a little frustration, but mostly we laugh it off and help push each other's bikes back up to dry land—in typical Harley fashion, there is no dealership within a million miles who has the part, knows what part we mean, knows what end of a motorcycle goes forward, or can give us any indication of how long it will be until we can get back on the road.

The local KOA is taken over as temporary headquarters. I use the down time to call my wife and get a lot of writing done, and so does Matt, who by now has decided to write his own piece about the experience. Hopefully he finishes it, 'cause I'd like to read it myself. It's a calm quiet break from the constant forward motion of the last few days. Give in to the process of the campground. Collect firewood, fill water, set up tents, kick boots off, eat something, sleep in the sun, disconnect from the cycle of time. No rush, no stress—all is well, and as it must be.

The endless need to control and to attach ourselves to expectation becomes a strain on the soul, a non-stop machine of sorrow and frustration. Things are what they are. Actions have to be performed for the sake of doing them, and not because we are so tied up in the outcome of them that when it doesn't go our way we lose our shit. This is not to say we should not strive for glory—only that the glory must come from the deed itself, the performance of our duty—always choosing the interesting road, the most challenging endeavor, the highest risk. We pit ourselves against life as a challenge, but not one in which we need to control every outcome.

The doing must be sufficient. The road walked to take the step we are currently taking and not to drive ourselves to distraction by thinking about the next one. Rooted in the moment, our planning must be fluid and take the form of a strategy, a lifestyle, rather than a rigid set of plans that have not accounted for all the currents in the stream.

JULY 18, 2017. DAY 17.

Spent the early hours of the day sorting out tow and insurance garbage for the broken down bike, and its rider went with it some 75 miles away to have it fixed, and would ride back to meet us afterward.

Used the setback productively, drank black coffee and wrote, kicked back and thought about the finer things. Behind it all was a kind of bittersweet ache that only long periods away from home and loved ones can produce, something that I've never felt before this time around.

I spent my younger years in bad scenes with broken women, breaking them even worse on the false promises of hope and love, like a false lighthouse on shores of sharpened flint. Often, it was the other way around, prolonged stab wounds to my guts with the blade of betrayal, infidelity, dishonesty. All of my relationships were alleyway murders or suicide pacts, long and slow and painful as hell, dying from a stomach wound in a dumpster. Lonely and harsh and awful.

Figuring things out later in life, realizing that your youth and pride and bullshit were all in the way of knowing anything, seeing anything for what it was. Love ain't dead, we just kill it little by slow with hard liquor, filthy hearts and hollow words.

Rode into the night down to dread Lemuria, leaving the 101 behind after frustration with the driving abilities of tourists in RV's ruined our vibe. Made the hard choice to forsake seeing the redwoods and cut down the 5 into California to make up for all the lost time, as Sam had a date he had to make in Tucson to pick up his old lady from the airport.

I lived here for a while in my late teens, in northern California near Mt. Shasta, from the time I was 15 till just after my 17th birthday. It was a mixed bag of things. The first time I had lived away from all my brothers, and was really "on my own," as my brother was locked up and doing his first stretch of time as a juvenile.

It was out here that I started a relationship with weight training and competitive sport (I played hockey, but preferred the fighting to the playing and never became that competent), had my first real girlfriend, and started really developing an idea of who I wanted to be. I'd say at 15, despite the youthful ignorance, I had some kind of eye on destiny already, and most of the things that I got into then are things I still appreciate now.

I read a lot of formative texts back then, like most guys in their teens, and started writing more—in essence, I wasn't born until I had to create myself rather than living in my older brother's shadows. For that reason, California holds some kind of significance to me still as being linked with my first voyage into the unknown frontier, and here I was again, riding those hot dusty roads.

It's funny how a physical place can collapse time. Cruising through Redding, I am fifteen again, and not a day has passed. Drinking beer on overpasses with Sam and Nate Carnes and Dan Baker (wherever he is now, I hope he's well) and pissing on cop cars, walking to the coffee shop to write and avoid being home. The smell of my girlfriend's Jeep as we ride around aimlessly, Type O Negative playing on the stereo while she smokes clove cigarettes like the girl in the song—she reaches for my hand and I pull it away. I haven't even told her I am leaving for good next week. A million experiences I have forgotten about for 16 years, all rush back and are new again.

There is a sorrow beneath it all, wide and pervasive, like an underground sea beneath a city on the plains. All the mistakes, all the regrets that we drive from our minds. There is too little time to dwell on these things, and casting our gaze backward through the years is a luxury for the old. The throttle is my friend, and I twist it, and

the years fall away, and I am back in the now— old loves turn to dust, old friends' names fade into nothing, old hurts return to scar tissue you can't even remember how you got. Burn it all.

Roll into Mount Shasta city at zero dark thirty, fried from the sun and lost in our own reveries.

JULY 19, 2017. DAY 18.

EVEN THE GRAFFITI in this town says things like "Namaste," or "Just Be Yourself."

We are not feeling the peace and love, and the tension between the crew keeps on growing throughout the day. Shit talk and anger nearly come to blows a few times, and the anger can be felt even in the way we ride—the distance becomes further and further between each rider and it eventually turns into a solo affair.

Suits me just fine, and I take my time, stop where I feel like it, and the desert envelops us as we cross into Nevada. The sky is something apocalyptic, wildfires in the area turning it into a smoky grey with the sun dull and distant. The wind is a blast furnace, stripping the moisture from mouth, nose and eyes faster than you can take it in, and getting stuck out here would be a real concern. This is a barren landscape, and I begin to feel as though I am on another planet as the smoke thickens and erases the horizon— there is nothing but the motorcycle, the road, the self. All else is desert and smoke.

I think I might be hallucinating as out of nowhere a body of water appears—expansive, vast.

The shores of Lake Walker are something out of a science fiction novel and do nothing to dispel the otherworldliness of the place. I stop my bike and enjoy the martian environment, ash and dust swirling in slow motion. Our Prospect, Pest, has joined up with me here, and we share some conversation and perspective on things.

A new addition to our crew, Pest is an ex-military mechanic who's been all over the world. He rides his bike like a bat out of hell, and adheres strongly to the principles of "Speed and Freedom."

Quick minded and good humored, Pest has a writer's heart and eye and imagination, and because of this, sees life as one big adventure, and he's looking to make himself a big character in it.

This is a guy who looks and vibes like you could've read about him in a Kerouac book, young face but an old heart, face impassive as he surfs by me on his Dyna down some lonesome highway at 4 in the morning.

Pest won't die of old age.

Tonopah rises from the desert like a city out of Arabian nights, the craggy rock that it is cradled in seeming to take forever to reach, the highway leading to it in a straight shot for miles and miles.

Rain is threatening, but the crew is divided, as usual, on who wants to stop where and when. Some of us want to call it a day and hit a motel for a hot shower after a long day of desert riding, and others want to press on. Arguing ensues, the other team wins, and we keep going into the desert night.

Riding on, the roads here have been washed out by recent flooding and I almost go down hitting a patch of wet sand and debris in the middle of the night. At some point we pull off the road and try to camp and I fall into a cholla cactus, getting a legful of painful needles. Tempers flare again, and we just keep on the throttle like junkies. We lose each other in the black.

We find each other again and tensions ease, beers are shared and we sleep with the scorpions in the middle of nowhere. I am reminded of Uncle Charlie, and my own zodiac symbol, the Scorpion, and I take it as a good omen.

"From the world of darkness I did loose demons and devils in the power of scorpions to torment."

JULY 20, 2017. DAY 19.

WOKE UP IN THE DIRT, desert sun already rising hot as it gets, and we lit out on our road with it baking down, cracks in the desert spreading out from us to the horizon, everything brown and beige and tan and dry. Reflections off chalk white sandstone bluffs so bright the tears start from your eyes, dries the sweat as fast as it pulls it from you—a thirsty, giant red vampire out in the void of space, pulling all water to itself and leaving you parched and dead or dying. Never enough water, can't drink it fast enough to keep up, and the whole ride is just thirst and burn.

Somewhere we came across a hot spring, where someone has carved a big rectangular swimming pool into the limestone, leaving the white dust in big piles. The spring ran down from a high hill covered in mesquite and cholla, the water steaming in the scored path, cooling slowly till it reached a tolerable heat in the pool, before running out the deep end and off into nowhere.

An empty light fixture stares down at us as we strip and simmer in the pool, with a sticker inside that reads "explore everything." Even in the heat, the natural hot tub rinses and cooks the miles away, and stepping out lets the breeze cool your skin down—the restoration is tangible, and the vultures seem disgusted.

The rest of the day is a blur. Ash springs, death towns, stress, heat, hell-holes, nuclear testing sites, no gas for miles, water on cracked lips, ragged scream of a desert bird, nightfall. We pull into some camp ground and argue with the guy who says we can't stay because of the flooding danger.

We ride on to Gila Springs, and grab a hotel. I sat in the parking lot for an hour or so, smoking cigarettes and sipping real cold beer, staring at a big saguaro cactus under neon lights and watching truckers pull in and out of the truck stop, big rigs howling off into the night. I realize I'm over it. I don't give a single fuck about being out here, it's all evaporated out of me. My mind has been a blank haze for days, and I am thinking a lot about Virginia, and all the things I have to do when I get back. My mind crosses a pivotal track and the trip is over for me, mentally. It has reached its termination point in my mind with thousands of miles to go yet.

I finish a six pack and fall asleep in the parking lot, and wake up not sure of where I am, or how long I slept.

JULY 21, 2017 DAY 20

BREAKDOWN in the brutal heat sixty miles outside of Tucson, AZ—the city that marks the end/beginning of the last/next leg of the trip. Dune. Arrakis. Desert planet. Heat waves ripple up from the black tar highway. Everything looks like an oil slick, or the inside of a glass of scotch and water. Dog goes limping off in the distance and I can't see anything, it's so bright.

I'm not even here anymore.

We make it to Tucson hours later and soak the weary away in the in-ground pool.

JULY 22, 2017 DAY 21.

IN LIFE, the weird times, the bad times, the wild times—they last the longest in our minds, clinging on forever like snakeskin that won't quite shed. The good times, the calm times, the peaceful ones—they seem to evaporate as soon as they're had, sort of like when you wake up and have the dream still in your mind—the harder you try to remember all the details, the more elusive they become, until they're just not there anymore.

Tucson was like that. Pool, sun, rainstorms, idle talk. My jones to be back on the road is real, highway junkie looking for a fix. Really though, truthfully, I just want to be home. It's nothing cool, or complicated. I'm tired. My tolerance level for the human race is on "E," and even friends are unwelcome intrusions into my little world. I just want to lose it all out there on the blacktop, all the chatter, the thoughts of past and future, the uncertainties when I get home, every scrap of who I am and where I've been.

In a lot of ways, this trip was about that the whole time. All the decisions you make in life that hem you up, or get you stuck in a web of interconnected responsibilities and judgements—the inability to really recreate yourself, or rewind and destroy. The urge to get up and go and leave behind, never come back, never look over your shoulder. Ecstasy is forgetfulness—that sweet nepenthe. We all build monoliths of past mistakes. Ruins of regret and bad choices, these towering monuments to human failure that make up the backdrop of every human life.

I see myself in the eye of a vulture as he swoops down across the road between Tucson and Tartarus. There's a tree, and a rope, and I'm swinging in the breeze. "Here's Luck," says the tattoo down my shin, with a man hanged above it. Everything collapses together and I can see where it begins and ends, and none of it really matters a bit.

JULY 23, 2017 DAY 22.

WE MAKE IT over to Sierra Vista, south of Tombstone. Some friends have a place there, and I need to change my oil and do some maintenance. A long day of vintage whiskey, Manowar and laughs ensue, but we are too tired to enjoy much of it. Falling asleep on my feet, and zoning out.

There's some issue with my brother's cell phone, and my friend's girlfriend, who is coming to see him, has her flight delayed in Phoenix. It looks like we won't be leaving Tucson for at least another day, and my brain revolts.

Some kind of claustrophobia, feeling other people's schedules and issues and timeframes and ideas closing in around me, I start to get cagey. I make my mind up to leave Sierra Vista in the morning on my own and push on through New Mexico into Texas. I need some kind of separation from the others, a severance with everything. I've got that old well known sadness rising up in my being, and wake up in the morning with it crushing my chest.

JULY 24, 2017. DAY 23

MANIC DEPRESSION, they used to call it.

The black dog. The blues. A big weight like a stone that comes unexpected and obliterates like Apophis, out of the blackness of space. Not a darkness that takes over, but a pervading sense of grey as a tangible thing, felt, all the way to the furthest horizon. Bleak, and devoid of possibility. It is relentless, and attacks by suffocation.

I'm in the grip. Packing up gear in the morning, I just want to lay back down and die—but I don't. I know Matthias will be pissed that I made the decision to move on ahead, and I can't make myself give a single fuck about it. They'll live. It's my life to live, and not theirs. I'm consumed by self, and my own worries and problems and despairs eclipse friendship and brotherhood and I am a solitary wanderer on the black tides of the void.

We are killing miles and killing time—Pest has come along with me, trying to get back to Nashville for his own reasons. New Mexico flies by, and we are in Texas. A Harley Dealership in El Paso to replace some parts that are falling off my bike—small repairs and we are back on the road, and looking across the Rio Grande to Ciudad Juarez, one of the bloodiest cities in the world.

Todestrieb is a German word that means "death drive." In French, they call it "L'appel du vide," or, "the call of the void."

Freud and other psychiatrists believe that there is an impulse in humans toward their own destruction—Thanatos directly opposed to Eros, or the desire to survive and live. You can feel it when some unexplained force pulls at you to rip the steering wheel directly into oncoming traffic, or jump off a building when you are standing at the edge. It can make the human act counter-intuitively, and denies the very instinct of self-preservation—I can feel it pumping through my veins like black oil.

Pushing the Harley to its limit, pinning the throttle, hearing the engine "ping" as it is overworked, switching lanes fast, slicing the highway up like a scalpel, letting go of the handlebars and feeling the bike pull hard one way or the other, delirious and seeing how far you can let it do its own thing before *Homo sapiens* programming takes over and I grab the bars before the edge of the road, heart pounding, skin electric from the wash of endorphins, adrenaline crackling up my spine.

Somewhere in this reckless activity, the embers smoulder. The thought that it is better to be alive than dead. It is just an abstract, but I've felt it a thousand times as the mind makes war with despair, and begins to win—through action, and the flirtation with death, the coals smoke.

Once we are back out on the rocky plains outside of El Paso, the rain that has dogged us the entire trip is back with a vengeance. Huge, pissed off storm clouds black out the desert sun.

You can see the rain falling in sheets as it comes toward you over the dust—lightning strikes from ground to sky, and a hawk screams and flies straight up into it as we scream into the rain at 100 miles an hour. The image burns itself into my mind, and the nature of it starts my mind thinking of big stories, legends, and things worth living for.

This is how it goes, in cycles. Soaring highs, and soul-crushing lows. No in between, no balance, no warning. My life has always been huge peaks and valleys deeper than the Mariana Trench. It's ok—I've gotten a certain sense of comfort in knowing that this won't change, it just has to be navigated. A reason has to be remembered and clung to like a buoy in the deep ocean, or you just drift away. Maybe it wins in the end, maybe I win—but I think that no matter who is the winner, it ends the same way.

Nothing is bigger or more lonesome than Texas at night on the silent highway.

We pull off on an exit ramp just outside of Colorado City, Texas, about 690 miles from where we started in the morning. We talk about where to stop, or what town to stay in, and decide to push on through or a while. While we talk, we both pause, and a comet burns its way through the night sky, closer than anything I've ever seen—it gets bigger and bigger, and finally burns out right over Colorado City. Must be a sign from the gods. We stop. We sleep.

JULY 25, 2017. DAY 24.

MADE IT TO FT. WORTH. Don't remember much of the ride from Colorado City, other than it was hot.

Once in Ft. Worth, we stopped in at Terry Shank's house, where we hung out with him and his Sergeant Jaws, drank a few beers, talked about the state of motorcycle culture, knives, fights and all that good stuff. Around evening, we went back to Terry's forged, picked out some steel and watched him forge a knife, listening to his blacksmith wisdom, and how the whole process works of taking a lump of atoms and re-ordering them into something that will take a life.

An interesting guy with a great talent and a lot hospitality. I reckon we will see each other again before this is all over. Stayed up till 2 or 3 am in the forge, and finally crashed out to the sound of Terry's pet rabbit scrabbling around the house.

: KNIFE, WEAPON, WILL :

: IRON AND BLOOD : ARE AT THE START -
KENAZ SPAWNED FROM CENAZ -
WHAT YOU HAVE - HOLD !
FEHU INTERTWINED WITH GROWTH -
THE REAPING GLEAM -

XCII/92
:92:

JULY 26, 2017, DAY 25.

GOT UP SUPER LATE and burned out of there with a note of farewell left behind and into Texarkana, Creedence's "Cotton Fields" playing over and over in my mind.

Swift trucks are the craziest drivers in America.

Met up with a few wayfarers somewhere on the road through here, too tired to make conversation, and they rode with us till somewhere around the Tennessee border.

An undeniable force kept pushing us. Tennessee was close enough to Virginia that it smelled like home, and I knew I couldn't stop for long till I was there.

By midnight, we hit Nashville, and Pest flashed me a raised salute, carving off on his own path now. We'd made it 700 miles since noon, and I didn't look back, kept on toward that black horizon.

Around 2am, the rain hit me again, my kickstand fell off, some kind of electrical thing was causing my lights to come off and on intermittently, I was deliriously tired, cold, pissed off, and out of it.

JULY 27, 2017. DAY 26.

FILLED MY TANK up and started to zone out on my feet. Raining on me still.

Wrapped up in a tarp, threw some trash bags down on the grass on the roadside and fell asleep for 30 minutes. Got up, drank some shitty gas station coffee. My brother calls. The crazy bastards have ridden non-stop since Cross Plains, Texas, and have passed me while I slept.

I'm in a bad way. Not sure where I am or who I am or what my name is and struggle through a phone call, angering my brother in the process. He hangs up on me while cussing me out, which bothers me a lot more than it should.

The relationship is hard to explain. Matt and I have lived our whole lives both probably feeling like we were living a little bit in the other's shadow at times. Big personalities, big egos, big dreams and plans, but inseparable and insanely loyal to each other in a way that I reckon few others have, or could ever understand.

Matthias is a force of nature. Larger than life, a raging temper and a crazy laugh, both moods passing like sudden storms, but a more grounded guy now, in his thirties—but I'm watching him come apart again in the current situation. A fifteen year marriage ending, and nowhere to really go, or be, and I feel like I'm letting him down in some way by not being able to help him more.

The living embodiment of Conan, Matt has always been popular with the ladies, and quick with his fists.

He's been a drug dealer, streetfighter, poet, artist, repo man and inmate. He's had a lot of friends, and his only real long term enemy is boredom, which he combats with a vengeance, by living life to the hilt and always voraciously looking for "the next one."

There's more to say about him and the wild times we've had together that would fill a much bigger book than this one, but you'll be able to hear him tell those stories in his own books, or maybe one day I'll write one about him.

A lot of people have called him a lot of things, but I just call him my older brother.

I know the storm will blow over, and I mostly just care about getting back home in one piece.

I saddle up again, holding my kickstand up with a bungee cord and jury rigging the wiring again so the lights remain on. I am almost to Virginia, and my bike can fall apart once I get there, but not yet.

I open the throttle and start slaughtering the miles.

So close to the Virginia border, and there's the blue lights flashing next to me, Tennessee Highway Patrol angrily motioning for me to pull   over.
I didn't know how fast I was going because I don't run a speedo.

Couldn't see him in the rear view because I don't run mirrors.

Wasn't listening to him as he started telling me he was taking me to jail because I was too damn tired.

Apparently I was doing 25 over, and in the state of Tennessee, "boy, you gotta play by our rules or we'll throw your ass in jail, y'hearme?"

Another cop pulls up and they go back and forth about taking me in or not. I call my brother and he's cool. They are 30 minutes down the road, and he tells me he's got my back and bail and all that, and I feel like catching up to those dudes and giving 'em a hug.

Sam and Matthias are the best friends on the planet. I miss 'em.

The cops decide not to take me to jail, but hit me with three massive tickets, give me hell about the mirrors till I tape my phone to my bars with the "reverse" camera on to satisfy them it works like an electronic mirror, and they follow me for 20 miles because there are no real crimes being committed somewhere else in Tennessee, I guess.

I cannot understand the mentality that makes a guy want to become a law enforcement worker. "Keeping people safe," they say, while they pull you over for inspection stickers, registration tags, no seatbelt, probable cause, whatever, and extort money from you for the government.

That kind of person will always be another breed from me, and might as well be a different species. From where I'm standing, I've never had much good experience with a police officer, and I don't expect I ever will.

A few miles on, the smokies are finally done following me and I reunite with what's left of the crew and we catch up a little bit. Share a few of the sketchier moments since we last saw each other. There's just three of us left to make the last little stretch of what has been one hell of a pilgrimage.

We put the hammer down.

Rain storms, insane rain like I've only seen in the South but imagine feels like Viet Nam or Thailand. Just blinding sheets of rain, falling so hard that cars pull off, the sides of the road like rivers, thunder, lightning, the whole 9 yards. The Old Dominion, Virginia, brings us back like she sent us off. Crossing the border back into Virginia, there's a tangible relief. It's finally over. 4 weeks has felt like 4 years, and I am different. I can't say how, yet, but a change has occurred.

It's a cold day, and the rain doesn't quit. We briefly pull of under an overpass, and then decide, fuck it, what's the point? We are two hours from home.

In Bedford, we part ways again.

By the time I pull into the trips final destination I feel like I'm catching hypothermia from the cold and wet and speed—I've been holding the throttle down and screaming against delirium and the weather and the wind and road and every other fucking thing on this planet, in this solar system, galaxy, universe, multiverse. Roaring at the very fabric of reality, all the thoughts I've had out here on this seemingly endless road coming together at the highway's end like the point of a spear, and jamming straight into the unblinking eye of god.

I'm cutting off a big rig and passing a sign that says "Lynchburg." I'm not ready to be home yet, all of a sudden. I pull off the road and out of the rain, finally, at a Holiday Inn, and check in. Hot shower. Look at my face in the mirror, looking thin and tired, hair shaggy, lines starting to relax.

I pick up the phone and call my old lady, and tell her where to come see me.

Home, now that it's so close, can wait.

EPILOGUE: AN EXHORTATION TO ADVENTURE

LIFE DOESN'T happen at home, or on the couch. Sure, you have to exist there at various times, but the stories you'll tell to future generations, or that will be told about you are unlikely to come from long periods of sedentary habit. If you are feeling the need to experience the open highway, the silent woodlands, or the exotic allure of a foreign land—do yourself a favor and start working toward that goal, that next great adventure RIGHT NOW.

None of us know how many more wake-ups we have left, how many more "I love you's" or solitary, quiet mornings spent watching the sun rise over the endless waves of the ocean.

We get one life, not several. Whatever you choose to believe, this life, the one that is moving by right now, is the one you've got to work with.

In our day and age, a cross continental motorcycle trip can be done with a few hundred bucks in gasoline and a good tent. A plane ticket to somewhere you've never seen before: a few hundred bucks and some networking to stay someplace or just camp out there, too.

The experiences and stories you will place yourself into when you opt to hit the open road are priceless, and together they weave the wild tapestry of our saga here, the only kind of immortality we can attain. Don't wait for the perfect moment—make it.

I hope that as soon as you get done reading this, you pick up a map, crank up your motorcycle, buy a plane ticket, and head to someplace you've never been; talk to strangers, get lost, perform a ritual known only to you at some mountain river that you don't know the name of, go off the beaten path, take a chance, and come home to recharge and do it all again. Or maybe, if it suits you, to never come home at all.

· MOTORCYCLE ·
· WHEEL / FREEDOM ·

:MOTORCYCLE
WHEEL
FREEDOM:

TRUE FREEDOM IS :POWER: AND
UNRESTRAINED MOVEMENT-
FTW

51533386R00107

Made in the USA
San Bernardino, CA
01 September 2019